READING AND MAKING NOTES

POCKET STUDY SKILLS

Series Editor: ***Kate Williams****, Oxford Brookes University, UK*
Illustrations by Sallie Godwin

For the time-pushed student, the *Pocket Study Skills* pack a lot of advice into a little book. Each guide focuses on a single crucial aspect of study giving you step-by-step guidance, handy tips and clear advice on how to approach the important areas which will continually be at the core of your studies.

Published

14 Days to Exam Success (2nd edn)
Analyzing a Case Study
Blogs, Wikis, Podcasts and More
Brilliant Writing Tips for Students
Completing Your PhD
Doing Research (2nd edn)
Getting Critical (3rd edn)
How to Analyze Data
Managing Stress
Planning Your Dissertation (2nd edn)
Planning Your Essay (3rd edn)
Planning Your PhD
Posters and Presentations
Reading and Making Notes (3rd edn)
Referencing and Understanding Plagiarism (2nd ed[illegible]
Refle[illegible]riting (2nd edn)
[illegible]ting (2nd edn)
[illegible]tudy Skills
[illegible]g with Dyslexia (2nd edn)
[illegible]ess in Groupwork (2nd edn)
[illegible]uccessful Applications
Time Management
Using Feedback to Boost Your Grades
Where's Your Evidence?
Writing for University (3rd edn)

POCKET STUDY SKILLS

Jeanne Godfrey

READING AND MAKING NOTES

THIRD EDITION

BLOOMSBURY ACADEMIC
LONDON • NEW YORK • OXFORD • NEW DELHI • SYDNEY

BLOOMSBURY ACADEMIC
Bloomsbury Publishing Plc
50 Bedford Square, London, WC1B 3DP, UK
1385 Broadway, New York, NY 10018, USA
29 Earlsfort Terrace, Dublin 2, Ireland

BLOOMSBURY, BLOOMSBURY ACADEMIC and the Diana logo are trademarks of Bloomsbury Publishing Plc

First published in Great Britain 2010

This edition published 2023

Cover design: eStudio Calamar

A catalogue record for this book is available from the British Library.

A catalog record for this book is available from the Library of Congress

ISBN: PB: 978-1-3503-2185-4
ePDF: 978-1-3503-2191-5
eBook: 978-1-3503-2190-8

Series: Pocket Study Skills

Typeset by Integra Software Services Pvt. Ltd.
Printed and bound in India

Contents

MAKING NOTES

Acknowledgements

My thanks go to all my students, past and present and future for helping me develop insights into reading and making notes.

I am grateful to Kate Williams for asking me to write this book and for her continuing support. I would also like to thank Sallie Godwin for her excellent illustrations.

Thanks also to Helen Caunce and Emma Pritchard at Bloomsbury, to Deborah Maloney at Integra and Maggie Lythgoe for her eagle-eyed copy-editing.

The extract from the Food Standards Agency (FSA) report on nutritional labelling is reproduced with the kind permission of the National Heart Forum. The article extract by Andrew Oswald is reproduced with the kind permission of Wiley-Blackwell Publishing.

Introduction

Reading and making notes are fundamental to studying at university, and this pocket guide will take you through the key points of these two processes quickly and clearly. Confidence comes from knowing *what* to do and *how* to do it, but when you start out at university you may not know exactly what is expected of you. Some commonly held misconceptions about university study are listed below.

Ten myths about reading and making notes at university

#1 You need to read most things on your reading list, starting at the top and working your way down.

#2 The best way to find your own sources is by using Google and Wikipedia.

#3 You need to read the text carefully from start to finish.

#4 Reading quickly is the most time-effective strategy.

#5 As you read, you should look up all the words you don't understand.

#6 You can't criticise what an academic text says because you are not an expert.

#7 Intelligent people understand a text straight away.

#8 You don't need to make notes, you can just annotate, copy and paste.

#9 Effective notes have all the points from the text copied down.

#10 Making notes in lines and columns is the best technique.

This pocket guide will show you why these ideas are incorrect and what you can do instead to meet your tutor's expectations and use your reading and notes effectively and successfully. *Reading and Making Notes* gives you practical advice and uses real assignment titles, reading lists and text extracts. It also uses real university marking criteria and tutor feedback.

Reading and note-making at university can be enjoyable, and I hope that using this pocket guide will help you to feel more confident and relaxed about these aspects of your work. I want you to be able to hit the ground running from the very start of your studies, to get the best marks possible for your work and make the best possible use of your talents, your tutors and your time.

PART 1

NOW YOU ARE AT UNIVERSITY ...

1 Active reading and note-making

At university, you need to 'move up a level' in terms of how you approach your reading, how you *think* about what you read, and how you make and use notes that reflect and enhance these deeper thinking processes.

At school/college	At university
Your reading material* is usually set and managed by the teacher.	Apart from a few key texts*, *you* are expected to decide what to read and what not to read.
All the students on a course read the same texts.	You choose what to read, so some of your sources* will be different from those of the other students, even if you are all doing the same assignment.

At school/college	At university
Students learn mainly by absorbing the information in the texts and repeating it in different forms.	You are expected to make up your own mind about *whether, why* and *how* the ideas in the literature* are important. Therefore, what you write about in relation to your reading texts will be unique to you.
Although there are different reasons for making notes, the main purpose is to record information and ideas.	At university, there is a much wider range of reasons for making notes. One of the key purposes is to help you develop and record a clear picture of your individual understanding, analysis and evaluation of a text.

* Throughout this book I use the terms *material, sources* and *texts* interchangeably to refer to any type of written, visual or spoken document. The term *literature* refers to all the material within an academic discipline or subject.

Having an active approach

We can summarise the points above by saying that at university you are expected to be an *active scholar* and take responsibility for your own learning. Rather than just learn and then reproduce an idea or piece of information, you are expected to understand and then analyse, question and evaluate it. Importantly, you can't do these things in a vacuum; they can only be done in relation to your own context – your current knowledge, ideas and worldview.

So, the main point of university study is to examine and apply your own thinking to current knowledge and, in doing so, produce new data, insights, ideas, theories or solutions that constitute new knowledge.

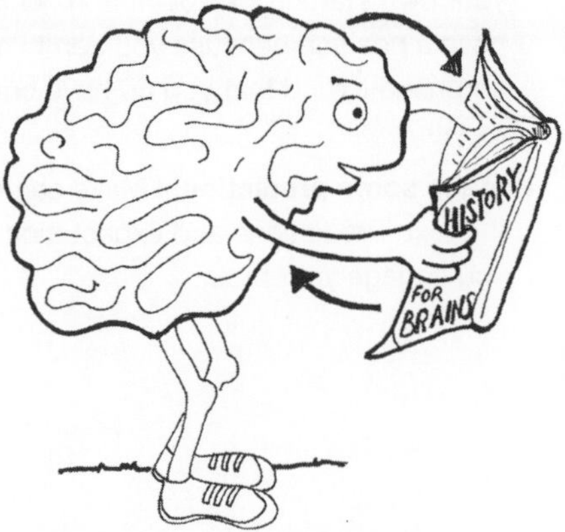

Below are strategies to help you engage your brain by thinking about the information before, during and after you read and/or make notes.

Before

- **Have a clear purpose:** Think about whether, why and how you are going to read and make notes on a text. What questions do you hope to answer and what do you hope to learn?
- **Have your own starting point:** Think about what your own position is on the issue, as you won't be able to analyse or evaluate what you read unless you have your own starting viewpoint from which to do so. Don't worry if you think you don't have a position because you don't know anything about the topic – you will be surprised to find that you do have one, even if it is relatively basic or uninformed as yet.
- **Make some predictions:** Make some predictions about what you expect to find in the text. Predictions and expectations (even if they turn out to be wrong) will help you engage your brain.

During

- **Build a scaffold:** Try to link what you read to what you already know about the subject, how it relates to other topics and how it relates to your own life experience. Building this 'knowledge scaffold' will help you understand what you read more easily and effectively because you will have something on which to hang the new information.
- **Think about the author's context:** Someone wrote each text you read. Think about who they are, why they might have written their text and what you think they are trying to achieve.
- **Engage and enjoy:** Engage and interact with the text – there should be a continuous two-way process of reading and questioning, and putting together old and new information to create your own unique way of thinking. Question and challenge the author's points in your mind and react to what you read – you will enjoy it much more. (See Chapter 12.)

After

- **Review and rework:** Once you have read and made notes, review and reflect, and rework your notes into a summary, a critique or a different note format (see Chapters 16 and 19).

Build up your reading stamina

Reading and making notes purposefully and actively is hard work, and you will probably find it difficult at first. Have the confidence to know that you will develop your information scaffolds and subject knowledge. Texts that at first seem impossibly difficult and alien will become easier as you finish them and then go back to them after reading other material on the same topic. You will build up your 'reading muscles' by – you guessed it – reading!

PART 2

Reading

DECIDE *WHAT* YOU ARE GOING TO READ

2

What your lecturers are looking for

Producing an excellent assignment is a bit like building a house – you start with your interpretation of the design (your assignment title) and then build your house brick by brick (your paragraphs) using good quality materials (relevant and reliable sources) and your own building skills (your critical thinking and appropriate writing style). Your finished house will be a little different from everyone else's, even though you have all worked from the same original design brief.

The diagram on the next page uses a 'building a strong wall' analogy to show that you need to build upwards from the solid foundation of understanding your assignment title.

7 Persuade your tutor of your answer by using sources selectively as evidence in your assignment.

6 Use your understanding of the texts and your own thoughts on them to come to your own ‘answer’ to the assignment title.

5 Bring *yourself* to the text and decide what *you* think about the author’s message.

4 Understand what the author is trying to do in their text and how it compares and connects to the ideas of other authors on the topic.

3 Understand and reflect on what you read.

2 Decide which sources are relevant and reliable.

1 Understand your assignment title accurately and reflect on what *you* think about the issue.

Start here!

Below, grouped into these seven stages, are extracts from university marking criteria in the 'excellent' category. Words in bold are defined in Appendix 2.

'Excellent' category marking criteria ✓	
7	'evaluates evidence and **synthesises** material clearly to develop persuasive arguments' 'evidence used appropriately to support their conclusion'
6	'clear insight and independent thought' 'an accurate and critically reflective treatment of all the main issues'
5	'willingness to engage critically with the literature and ability to go beyond it' 'mindful of other interpretations'
4	'clear understanding of the nature of the material' 'ability to analyse materials and their implications'
3	'sources used accurately and concisely but do not dominate' 'good command of the literature'
2	'evidence of ability to select appropriately' 'detailed *and* broad knowledge base'
1	'has interpreted the question fully and accurately'

… and below, grouped into the same seven stages, are marking criteria extracts relating to poor assignments.

'Poor' category marking criteria ✗	
7	'**baseless assertions**' 'essay is overreliant on too few sources' 'poorly used material'
6	'uses mainly description rather than coming to a critical conclusion'
5	'does not go beyond the assertion of points derived from the literature'
4	'lack of awareness of the context of the material'
3	'inaccurate reading and limited understanding'
2	'needs to refer to the relevant literature' 'some sources used are not **academically rigorous**'
1	'has not clearly understood the assignment task'

3 Understand your assignment title

- ✓ 'has interpreted the question fully and accurately'
- ✗ 'has not clearly understood the assignment task'

Understanding your assignment title is crucial. Don't make the mistake of reading the title quickly, assuming you know what it means and then plunging into unfocused reading. Instead, make sure you have clearly identified and understood:

C: the **concept** words or phrases: words related to the content of the topic.

F: the **function** words: does the title ask you to describe, analyse, argue, or perhaps do all of these things?

S: the **scope** of the title: what you are asked to cover and not to cover. If this is not explicit in the title, you will need to decide on the scope yourself.

Use these three aspects to break down and examine your title. Discuss it with fellow students, and get advice from your tutor if you are not sure what it means.

Let's have a look at two real assignment titles and see how the student has used the C, F and S technique to understand them.

Assignment title 1

Course BSc Health and Human Sciences
First-year module 'Nutrition and Lifestyle'

Case study title

illness caused by lifestyle - e.g.
(C) coronary heart disease (CHD), diabetes 2.
I will choose CHD.

Your client has one of the major lifestyle-related diseases.

(F) brief summary only

Outline the aetiology of the disease and give a critical account of the measures that are being taken in your country to prevent it.

(F) Don't just describe! - how effective are they? Problems?

(C) causes

(C) actions e.g.
- policies
- legislation
- advice
- NHS/Schools...

(S) now (not past!)

(C) not worldwide U.S.A

Assignment title 2

Course MSc in Economic Psychology
Seminar series on 'Happiness and the Economy'

Essay title

To what extent is there a correlation between the economic performance of a society and the levels of happiness experienced by that society?

(C) clear/statistical link

(C) i.e. a nation's economic state

(F)
- if there is a correlation, how strong is it?
- are there any exceptions to such a link?
- what are the problems/issues with trying to find a correlation?

(S) which society/ies? I will choose Western/developed societies.

(C) how happy people are

For more help with assignment titles, see *Planning Your Essay* and *Getting Critical* in this series.

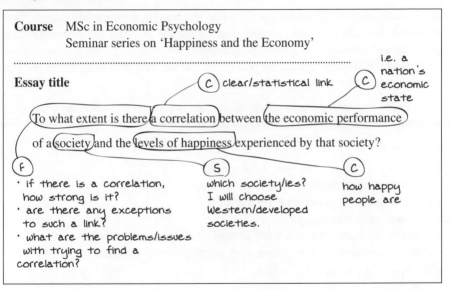

A clearer idea of what you need

Once you have analysed your assignment title, you need to ask yourself what *you* think about the issue, as you won't be able to question and evaluate source material and evidence without your own starting position from which to do so. Your viewpoint will (and should) develop and possibly change as you work on your assignment but you do need one to start with.

Having both your title and your own position clear in your mind should help you decide what type of information and evidence you need to find.

Think about:

- The *types* of sources you need, for example:
  - introductory textbooks
  - key established works on the topic
  - original data from experiments
  - recent academic journal articles on new developments or ideas
  - non-expert and/or public views from websites or newspapers.
- *Why* you need these types of texts.
- *How* you think you need to read these texts (e.g. read the whole text, just some sections, read quickly, read carefully).

- *What* questions you want answered as you read.

Thinking about why and how you will engage with reading material at this early stage is important – it will help you target your search and selection of sources and start you on your journey of producing a successful and original piece of work.

4 Take control of your reading list ...

Myth #1 **You need to read most things on your reading list, starting at the top and working your way down.**

Your tutors do *not* want you to read everything on the reading list – they want to see that you can select relevant material. Now that you have analysed your title, have your starting position and thought about what types of sources you need and why, take control of your reading list and decide what *you* want to read rather than letting your reading list control you.

! Two things to note about reading lists:

Tutors might list sources in alphabetical order of author, in date order, or in a random way, so do not assume that the list order should be your reading order.

Tutors do not always give the complete bibliographic details of texts, but you must find the full details of any source you use in your assignment and give these in your bibliography and/or reference list.

Let's look at the reading list for the first-year module 'Nutrition and Lifestyle' and see how you might assess whether any of the sources listed are relevant for assignment title 1 (see p. 12). Remember that the focus of the student's assignment is to critically evaluate the guidelines and actions being taken in the UK to prevent coronary heart disease.

For more on how to reference, see *Referencing and Understanding Plagiarism* and *Writing for University* in this series.

Reading list for the 'Nutrition and Lifestyle' module

The reading list below is for the module in general. You will also need to find some more specific sources for your chosen assignment topic (please see departmental Key Texts collection and ask your tutor for guidance if necessary).

Tutors will often give you useful advice at the top of a reading list.

The latest editions of *MAFF Manual of Nutrition*, Food Standards Agency, London.

The FSA (Food Standards Agency): www.food.gov.uk/

Scientific Advisory Committee on Nutrition (SACN): www.sacn.gov.uk

Scan these websites for latest government recommendations on dietary advice for preventing CHD.

Lanham-New S, Hill R, Gallagher A and Vorster H (eds) (2019) *Introduction to human nutrition* (3rd edn). Oxford: Wiley-Blackwell.

A basic textbook – check the chapter headings for those that are relevant to the assignment. Note that this is the 3rd edition – is this the latest one?

Graham JJ, Timmis A, Cooper J, Ramdany S, Deaner A, Ranjadayalan K and Knight C (2006) Impact of the National Service Framework for coronary heart disease on treatment and outcome of patients with acute coronary syndromes. *Heart*, 92(3): 301–6.

What is the National Service Framework? If it relates to your government's guidelines, then this article is probably relevant to the assignment.

Public Health England (2019) *Health matters: preventing cardiovascular disease.* https://ukhsa.blog.gov.uk/2019/02/14/health-matters-preventing-cardiovascular-disease/

This publication looks relevant.

Rauber F, Chang K, Vamos EP, da Costa Louzada ML, Monteiro CA, Millett C and Levy RB (2021) Ultra-processed food consumption and risk of obesity: a prospective cohort study of UK Biobank. *European Journal of Nutrition*, 60(4): 2169–80.

An article about obesity, so not directly relevant – just scan the abstract.

McArdle W, Katch V and Katch F (2018) *Sports and exercise nutrition* (5th edn). New York: Wolters Kluwer.

Not relevant to the assignment topic.

So, from this section of the module reading list, the student needs to read two or three websites, probably one chapter from the textbook and two journal articles.

You will probably need to find a few other sources yourself. Look at the assignment title again – what reading gaps do you need to fill? You probably need material that evaluates viewpoints on the effectiveness of measures to prevent heart disease.

Let's now take a look at the complete reading list for the MSc Economic Psychology seminar series and decide which sources are likely to be relevant for the assignment 2 title on page 12 about possible links between economic performance and happiness.

Reading list for 'Happiness and the Economy' seminar series

Basic reading

Take note of headings in your reading lists and read some of the 'basic' or 'essential' sources before moving on to those listed under 'additional' or 'extra' reading.

Durand M (2015) The OECD better life initiative: How's life? and the measurement of well-being. *Review of Income and Wealth*, 61(1): 4–17.

◄ Probably relevant, although the title indicates that the article is about measuring well-being rather than happiness per se – read the abstract to check for relevance.

Ferrer-i-Carbonell A (2013) Happiness economics. *SERIEs*, 4(1): 35–60.

Frey BS and Stutzer A (2010) *Happiness and economics*. Princeton, NJ: Princeton University Press.

◄ Both look relevant.

Weimann J Knabe A and Schöb R (2015) *Measuring happiness: The economics of well-being*. Cambridge, MA: MIT Press.

◄ Too general to be directly relevant, but check the chapter headings if you have time.

Argyle M (2001) *The psychology of happiness*. Departmental box.

Easterlin RA (2006) Life cycle happiness and its sources: intersections of psychology, economics, and demography. *Journal of Economic Psychology*, 2(4): 463–82.

EITHER

Myers DG (1994) Who is happy – and why? (Chapter 11 of *Exploring social psychology*) 2.930.

OR

Myers DG and Diener E (1995) Who is happy? *Psychological Science*, 6(1): 10–19.

Oswald AJ (1997) Happiness and economic performance. *The Economic Journal*, 107(445): 1815–31.

Might be relevant – scan to check, keeping the focus on economic performance and happiness.

Might be relevant – scan to check, keeping the focus on economic performance and happiness.

The tutor indicates that you only need to read one of these. Also note that these sources are quite old and think about why they might be on the reading list.

Looks relevant but again it is a relatively old source.

Additional material
Frey BS (2021) What future happiness research? In *A Modern Guide to the Economics of Happiness*. Cheltenham: Edward Elgar Publishing, pp. 17–27.
Hetschko C Knabe A and Schöb R (2020) Happiness, work, and identity. *Handbook of Labor, Human Resources and Population Economics*. Cham: Springer, pp. 1–26.

← This is about researching happiness – read abstract* to see if it is relevant.

← Happiness at work so not directly relevant.

So, from this reading list, you would probably need to read six or seven articles and quickly read the abstracts of a couple more sources to check for relevance. Note that as this is a Master's level course, you would also be expected to find some sources of your own (see Chapter 5).

* See glossary on p. 140.

Some other things to remember about reading lists

- Don't expect your tutor to tell you what to read. If you are unsure, do some thinking and selecting of possible sources and then ask your tutor what they think of your choices.
- You might get a well-ordered, detailed and helpful reading list or you might not – some lecturers expect you to do more detective work than others.
- Even within the 'required' or 'essential' reading list section, there may be titles that cover similar ground to each other, so still be selective.
- Reflect, even if only briefly, on *all* the titles on your list, even the ones you reject – this will help you to familiarise yourself with the expert authors in the field.
- Discuss individual texts with other students, but don't share your whole selection or the whole list of sources you have found yourself – this detective work will help make your assignment unique and it belongs to you alone.

5 ... and go beyond it?

- ☑ 'evidence of ability to select *appropriately*'
- ☑ 'good command of the literature'

When you have read your selected sources, there might still be some knowledge gaps you need to fill. Even for first-year assignments, your tutor will probably expect you to find one or two sources of your own. However, stick to the rule of only searching for sources once you have a clear idea of what you are looking for and why. If you feel that you have a good range of different viewpoints and suitable sources already, trying to find more material just for the sake of it will be a waste of time.

At higher levels of study (third-year undergraduate and postgraduate), finding source material is a key part of the academic research that will make your assignment unique. Going 'off-road' beyond your reading list will help you build up a good command of the literature and gain you marks.

Any source you find must be **relevant** and **reliable**. We will look at source reliability in Chapter 6. Let's concentrate for now on finding sources that are relevant, using the 'Nutrition and Lifestyle' module reading list. On p. 20 we identified that the student still needed sources that contained a critical evaluation of the measures being taken to prevent heart disease in the UK. Below is a selection of off-road sources a UK student found by using the search phrase 'effectiveness of preventive measures for CHD in the UK'. In the right-hand column are comments on the sources' relevance for this topic.

Off-road sources found for assignment 1

Ananthaswamy A (2004) Eat less and keep disease at bay. *New Scientist*, 2444: 11–12.

Bupa (n.d.) *Coronary heart disease*. www.bupa.co.uk/health-information/heart-blood-circulation/coronary-heart-disease

Davies R, Roderick P and Raftery J (2003) The evaluation of disease prevention and treatment using simulation models. *European Journal of Operational Research*, 150(1): 53–66.

Gemmell RF, Heller K, Payne K et al. (2006) Potential population impact of the UK government strategy for reducing the burden of coronary heart disease in England: comparing primary and secondary prevention strategies. *Quality & Safety in Health Care*, 15(5): 339–43.

'Disease' is too general and the article is not about government measures. Finally, *New Scientist* is not an academic source - not relevant.

About CHD so relevant (but not an academic source).

This is about disease in general, so only relevant if it discusses CHD in the UK.

Yes, this looks relevant, as it discusses the impact of UK government strategy to reduce CHD. NB Check what 'population impact' means.

Department of Health and Social Care (2000) *National service framework: coronary heart disease*. www.gov.uk/government/publications/quality-standards-for-coronary-heart-disease-care

National Health Service (n.d.) *Prevention: coronary heart disease*. www.nhs.uk/conditions/coronary-heart-disease/prevention/

Goenka S (2018) *Cardiovascular disease prevention in India*. www.mrc-epid.cam.ac.uk/wp-content/uploads/2018/07/Shifalika-Goenka_opt.pdf

About what measures the government is taking to prevent CHD and how to implement them, so relevant, although it will probably not contain evaluation.

Advice about preventive measures, so relevant, although probably no evaluation.

Preventive measures in India not the UK. So not relevant. Also, these are presentation slides, not a reliable academic source.

6 Reliable and academic sources

Myth #2 **The best way to find your own sources is by using Google and Wikipedia.**

Tutors tell students to use 'reliable', 'credible', 'authoritative', 'scholarly', 'academic' or 'academically rigorous' sources. These terms are often used interchangeably, although strictly speaking there is a degree of difference between *reliable/credible/authoritative* and *scholarly/academic/academically rigorous,* as explained below.

What is a reliable source?

A reliable, credible or authoritative source is one that we can assume contains fairly accurate and correct information because it is written by an expert in that field. For you to be able to judge whether a source you have found is reliable, you need to be able to identify:

- **The author or authors** (this can be an organisation)**:** If you don't know who wrote something or where it came from, you can't judge its degree of accuracy, objectivity or purpose. Keep this in mind when you are searching or reading online (see also pp. 34 and 35).

- **Date of publication:** Again, if you don't know when something was written, you can't judge its purpose, context or relevance. Your sources should usually be as recent as possible unless there is a good reason for using an older source, for example in order to understand the development of an idea.
- **Evidence of accuracy, balance and objectivity:** The author should be able to demonstrate that their text is objective, balanced, truthful and accurate. However, bear in mind that all sources will have some bias – they have been written by human beings, after all. Moreover, how you define 'reliable' will depend on the type of information you are looking for. If, for example, you need information about people's personal views on a current political issue, then social media and TV programmes will be reliable sources for this information.

Primary and secondary sources

Primary sources are the 'first-hand' or original source of information, such as an original experimental report, an interview or a driving licence. Secondary sources are those that use the original (primary) source of information; for example, an academic article that discusses data from someone else's experimental report, a news report that discusses what was said in an interview, or an email in which you give details about a driving licence.

Primary sources are more reliable than secondary sources, but for your assignments you will often be using some primary and some secondary sources – just be aware of the difference between the two. Also bear in mind that a text might be both a secondary source of some information (e.g. someone else's data that the author uses to build their argument) and a primary source of other things (e.g. the author's argument).

What is an academic source?

'Some sources used are not academically rigorous.'

An academic, academically rigorous or scholarly source is one that has been quality checked by experts in the field before publication – a process called 'peer-review'. Academic texts need to include references for any source material used so that the information can be checked, and are usually books or articles published in an 'academic journal' – a journal that sends articles out for peer-review before accepting them for publication.

So, academic sources are also reliable but not all reliable sources are academic. For example, reports from government departments and established bodies such as the World Health Organization are fairly reliable (although a report will have been commissioned by someone and so have some degree of bias) but they are not 'academic' or 'scholarly' unless they have been peer-reviewed.

Unreliable and non-academic source types

The source types listed below are generally **not** suitable for use in university assignments because their authorship is unknown and/or unreliable, and/or because the material they contain has not been peer-reviewed:

- Wikipedia: wiki articles are useful for gaining a basic understanding of something but are too general to use as a source and can also contain misinformation.
- Websites ending with *.com* or *.org*. However, government publications can be used if the authors are known and authoritative and references are included.
- Website texts that have elements of marketing or journalistic content. Words that might indicate this are *magazine*, *digest*, *personals*, *news*, *press release*, *correspondent*, *journalist*, *special report, company*, *classified* and *advert.*
- YouTube videos and TED talks, but these can be used if the speaker is authoritative and references are included.

- Presentation slides
- Blogs
- Newspapers: even quality papers such as *The Times*, *The Independent* and *The Economist*
- Magazines: even magazines such as *Newsweek* and *New Scientist*
- Academic conference proceedings
- Doctoral or master's theses: these are 'scholarly' but have not been peer-reviewed.

As we said on p. 30, you might need less reliable sources such as social media for your research; it's a question of knowing *where* a source comes from and thinking about *why* and *how* you want to use it.

Reviews and abstracts are not academic sources

These can be useful to give you a general idea of a text but are not acceptable academic sources in themselves.

- **Book or article reviews:** Reviews do not give detailed information and include the personal opinion of the reviewer.

- **Article abstracts:** these give the outline of the text and usually (but not always) the conclusion. Reading an abstract is a good way of deciding whether the article will be useful to you, but you will need to read the full text in order to analyse and evaluate the evidence and use the article as a source in your assignment.

Use academic search engines, gateways and databases

General search engines are not good enough

Typing a search word into a general search engine (e.g. Google, Bing, Baidu, DuckDuckGo) will return everything on the internet containing that word, starting with the most popular webpages – not a useful way of finding specific, credible and academic sources. Also be aware that there are websites that call themselves a 'research database' and/or use phrases such as 'research journal' and 'volume/issue number', but which are not, in fact, reliable academic sites. Using the subject gateways recommended by your tutors via the library is a quicker, more reliable way of finding credible sources.

Google Scholar is not enough (on its own)

Open metadata sources and search engines such as Google Scholar are useful, particularly if you want to find a source for which you already know the title or author. However, for many of these open web engines, it's difficult to enter specific queries and it is often unclear how the returns have been generated (e.g. a search algorithm might include your location). In addition, returns often miss out more recent sources and include material that has not been peer-reviewed. So, it's a good idea to also use a subject-specific gateway or database.

Use subject-specific gateways via your university library

These gateways (also known as 'databases') have sources that have been 'quality checked' and are therefore good for finding academic sources. Use the gateways recommended by your tutors and/or libraries. Gateways most suited to finding academic sources include: ACM Digital Library, EBSCOhost, JSTOR, Ovid, ProQuest, PubMed, ScienceDirect, Scopus, TRID, Virtual Health Library, Web of Science and Wiley Online Library.

> **TIP** Don't forget that a search engine is not a source – you can't give 'Google Scholar' or 'JSTOR' as a reference in your work.

Go to database training sessions

Go to workshops or lectures you are offered on your course about how to use search engines and databases, even if you think you won't learn anything – you will. In these sessions you will be shown which portals are most relevant for your subject and how to use them effectively, including how to use the words 'AND', 'OR' and 'NOT' (referred to as 'Boolean' operators) when typing search queries. This information will allow you to find the best sources for your assignments and will save you a lot of time throughout your academic career.

Take responsibility for the reliability of your sources

If you are using a website, check that you know who wrote it and when, and also who funds and supports the site. Use the 'home' or 'about us' tabs to find out who is behind the site and see if it has a Wikipedia entry you can read for further information. Think about what the author's purpose might be and what biases they might have.

In summary, make sure that you know the author of any source you use. No matter how or where you find something, it is *your* job to make sure you know who wrote it and why, and to determine whether it is reliable and/or academic. If you don't know who wrote something, you shouldn't use it as source material.

Make the most of your library

Your university library will offer workshops and advice sessions on how their catalogue system works, which sources and databases are most relevant for your subject and how to use them. The table below summarises some of the pros and cons of using your library.

Using your university library

Pros:

The library will have:

- A quiet, warm and comfortable environment in which to study away from distractions.
- A more informal and social space you can use to combine study and networking.
- Expert staff who can give you advice on finding relevant academic material.
- Hard and/or online copies of sources listed as 'essential' on course reading lists. If all copies are out on loan (this is quite common), staff can help reserve a copy and give you advice on alternative sources.
- Resources chosen by lecturers and therefore deemed to be reliable and/or academic.
- Staff who can help you borrow sources from other libraries and who can also help you set up a SCONUL account so that you can use the study space in other university libraries.
- Printed material (e.g. back copies of newspapers) not available online.

Cons:

It's not home.

- You have to get there.
- You have to go back there to return the hard copies you take out.

7 Fine-tune your selection

This is an important stage that will save you a great deal of time in the long run. Collect your selection of sources and give each one a job interview. Does it have the correct expertise, qualifications and experience for what you want it to do?

Read the title, contents page, headings and index of each source to narrow down the sections that are most relevant. You may feel that deciding *not* to read something is somehow being disrespectful to the author, but this is just how academic study works – you are simply identifying that what the author has written is not right for your particular job.

Source checklist

Before you start reading a source in detail, you should be able to answer the following questions:

- What type of source is it?
- Who wrote it, when and why?
- Who has it been written for?
- Is it up to date, relevant, reliable and academic – and if not, is that OK for how and why you want to use it?
- What is its overall function, for example to describe, explain or argue?
- Why are you going to read it – what exactly do you want to get out of it?
- Do you think it will support your conclusion or give a different viewpoint?

Create a research log

This will enable you to build up your personal research database, reference the source properly in your assignment and find the source again in the future.

Here is an example of a research log entry:

Source details Oswald AJ (1997) Happiness and economic performance. *The Economic Journal*, 107(445): 1815–31. **Main idea** That employment does affect happiness but less because of income and more because of the fact of having a job.	**Search and research details** Found on 1/6/2022 by uni infolinx > e journals > JSTOR > using search phrase 'economics and happiness'. Also a copy in library (ref. only): JE201.2

Your completed log is the first stage of your research – your own selection of sources that you know are right for the job. This search, selection and collection of material is unique to you and is an important stage in producing an original assignment.

Summary

- Your tutors give you assignments to see whether you have understood the point of an issue or question and whether you have engaged with it at a deep level.
- An excellent assignment is built properly, with a conclusion that is persuasive because it is based on the evidence of relevant and reliable sources.
- Select the sources from your reading list that *you* think are most relevant.
- Don't be afraid to reject sources for fear that you might be missing something – there is not enough time to read everything.
- It is *your* responsibility to check that your sources are relevant, appropriate and reliable for the type of information you need.
- Keep a research log and nurture a sense of ownership of your own collection of sources. This collection belongs to you and is the start of producing an original piece of work.

PART 3

DECIDE *HOW* YOU ARE GOING TO READ

8 Ways to read

Before plunging into reading, take a few minutes to think about the best order in which to read your texts that will maximise ease of understanding, motivation, interest and efficiency. One way you might order your reading is shown in this 'staircase' illustration.

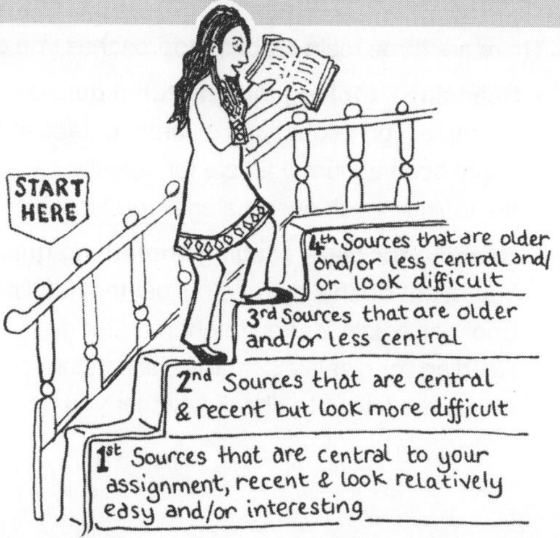

START HERE
4th Sources that are older and/or less central and/ or look difficult
3rd Sources that are older and/or less central
2nd Sources that are central & recent but look more difficult
1st Sources that are central to your assignment, recent & look relatively easy and/or interesting

Myth #3 **You need to read each text carefully from start to finish.**

There isn't enough time to read every source from cover to cover and you don't need to. We read things in different ways for different purposes – we quickly scan a train timetable for specific information, but we follow a recipe step by step. For academic study you should apply the same principle – matching the *way* you read something to *why* you are reading it.

There are three main reading approaches you can take:

- **Scanning – looking over material quickly to pick out specific information:** For example, you might scan a library database for texts on a specific topic, or you might scan a journal article for specific information. You might also scan when you are looking back over material you have already read in order to check something.
- **Reading for gist – reading something quickly to get the general idea and feel:** You might do this by reading just the headings, introduction and conclusion of a book, or article, or you might read for gist by going over the whole text quickly. Reading for gist is also called 'skimming' or 'reading for breadth'. An important use of gist reading is to check whether you need to read a particular text in detail.

- **Close reading – reading something in detail:** You will usually need to read key sources in detail in order to understand them completely and accurately. Close reading is also called 'deep reading', or 'reading for depth'. A popular method for doing close reading is to use the 'survey, question, read, recite and review' method, referred to as 'SQ3R'. You can also do 'text mapping' or use various visual and auditory reading strategies.

For more details about close reading techniques, see *Studying with Dyslexia* (pp. 74–83) in this series.

Reading on screen vs. reading on paper

Most of us read online a lot of the time, but when you need to do a detailed reading of a key text, there are real advantages to reading a hard (paper) copy.

Reading on screen	Reading from paper
Pros • Usually easier and cheaper. • You can customise, annotate, screenshot and copy and paste. • The text often has links to dictionaries and other material. **Cons** • You are likely to 'scroll and scan' rather than do deep, detailed reading. • Research shows that readers are more often distracted and read for less extensive periods (unless using an e-reader).*	**Pros** • People tend to remember more, possibly because paper texts give you a more sensory experience, leading to a higher level of engagement.* • Gives you a stronger sense of where you are in the text and of your progress. • You can text map – print and lay the pages out as a continuous scroll and then highlight headings and key sections, giving you are clear idea of the text's structure and argument development. • Portable, doesn't need power and you don't have to worry about damaging or losing your device.

Reading on screen	Reading from paper
• Readers are more likely not to know or forget the source of the text and to copy and paste, leading to a higher level of accidental plagiarism.* • Needs a power source.	**Cons** • You need an external light. • No direct links to other information.

* See Mangen et al. (2013).

TIP Whether you read from screen or paper, try to limit distractions (see p. 52), and when you need to do detailed reading, avoid letting your eyes continually skip ahead – you can use a piece of card or your finger to hide the lines below the one you are reading.

Stay flexible

You can, of course, combine screen and paper reading – you might want to scan or read sections of a text on screen and then print out or get hard copies to read the whole text in detail. You will also often need to use a combination of the three different reading approaches (scanning, gist and close reading) on one text. Finally, if you get a third of the way through a text and realise you are not getting what you want from it or can't understand it, zoom out to look at the overall structure of the text again and gist read it before going back to the detail. (See also p. 44).

Rereading

Sometimes, you will need to read a key text several times. Between readings, try to leave some time to consciously think about the text, and also to have some 'time out' (maybe a day or two) during which your brain will be working in the background, formulating your own ideas (see p. 84).

9 Finding the time to read

One reason for low assignment marks is that not enough time was spent on reading and thinking. Mild time pressure can increase your motivation and alertness, but too much pressure can lead to stress and rushed reading.

Here are some tips for planning your reading time:

- Plan to read at the times of day and week when you are most awake, alert and free from distractions.
- Have both a short-term (weekly) and a long-term (over a semester) reading plan.
- Plan reading sessions that strike a balance between being long enough for detailed reading and thinking, but not too long. For example: 30 mins reading > 5 mins break > 30 mins reading > 5 mins break > 30 mins reading > 5 mins break > and a final 20 mins thinking and writing about what you have read.
- Make sure family and friends understand that your university reading is demanding and important work and tell them (or even give them a copy of) your reading schedule.

Myth #4 Reading quickly is the most time-effective strategy.

How quickly should you be reading?

There is no precise answer to this question – understanding, questioning and reflecting on what you read is more important than speed. Try not to worry too much if your reading is slow at first – you will speed up as you become more familiar with the subject and its vocabulary. One tip is that if you are in the habit of reading sentences out loud (called 'vocalising'), try doing this a bit more quickly and in your head rather than aloud.

What about 'speed reading'?

There has never been good evidence that speed reading is effective, and research by Rayner et al. (2016) suggests that it does not work. The study shows that there is a trade-off between accuracy and speed, and that people who try to read too quickly do not understand much of what they read and do not remember the information well. Rayner et al. also show that people who claim to be good speed readers are usually very familiar with their topic and so can quickly scan a text and get a general idea of its content. The best reading strategy is to read well at your own speed and while doing so build up a solid knowledge of your subject and its vocabulary.

So how will you get through all the reading you have to do?

Everything we have covered in this book so far will help you deal with a large reading load, particularly:

- remembering that your tutors do not expect or want you to read everything (see p. 16)
- understanding your assignment title and then searching and selecting relevant sources (pp. 11–28)
- reading your texts in the most effective order (see p. 43)
- using different reading approaches effectively – scanning and gist reading some texts or text sections, leaving you time to read key texts in detail (see pp. 44–48)
- planning and managing your reading time (see p. 49).

The other important tool for coping with a large amount of reading is to make effective notes, and we will look at how to do this in Parts 5, 6 and 7.

Create the right environment

The right environment will help you read more effectively. Be aware of what might distract you – writing down a list of distractions and worries and the actions you can take to deal with them will help unclutter your mind. Also:

- Disable text notifications and/or turn off you phone.
- Make sure you have everything you need to hand.
- Ensure that you have adequate light (but without glare).
- Make sure your text is roughly at eye level so that you don't have to bend your neck.
- If you usually listen to music while studying but find that you can't focus when reading demanding university-level texts, try working without music.
- As mentioned in Chapter 6, remember that your university library can be a good place to read.

Most students find university-level reading tough at some stage, in terms of both difficulty and amount. It takes mental effort to select sources properly and to read key material carefully and critically – if your brain hurts a bit, then you are doing it right. However, if you find you really can't understand your texts, or you have continuous and/or increasing feelings of anxiety and of being overwhelmed, ask your tutors or student advisers for advice and help as soon as possible.

Summary

- You should *not* be reading everything on your reading list from start to finish.
- Decide why you want to read a text and what you want to get from it, and from this decide whether to scan, gist read or read it in detail.
- Spending time selecting the right sources and knowing which ones you want to just scan or gist read will leave you time to read key texts in detail.
- Review your progress as you read – if you are finding the text difficult, you might need to change your reading strategy or stop and read a different text.
- Try to plan your time so that you have enough time to both *understand* what you read and to *think* about it.
- Your reading environment should give you a balance between comfort and alertness.
- Your unique selection of sources belongs to you and is the start of producing an original assignment.

PART 4

UNDERSTAND, QUESTION AND EVALUATE WHAT YOU READ

10

Understand the text accurately

You need an active reading approach in order to understand, analyse and evaluate a text, so before reading the rest of this chapter, you might want to have a quick look back at Chapters 1 and 2 to remind yourself of what active reading entails.

Understanding texts

Let's look at the features present in most types of text that can help you understand them.

Have a look at Extract 1 below, which comes from a report written on behalf of a UK government body (the Food Standards Agency) in 2013, titled *Front of pack nutrition labelling: joint response to consultation.* A student found this source for the assignment about preventing lifestyle diseases such as coronary heart disease (see p. 12).

Here are some of the thoughts, ideas and predictions the student made about the topic and the text before they started reading, followed by the report extract itself.

I read some food labels and I know the basics of the colour-code (CC) system and use it sometimes when I buy food (I think it's quite good) but I want to know how exactly the FSA decided on the different colours.

I read the intro. when I selected this report and know that it is a govt dept (FSA) responding to a consultation to justify (I think) its own food labelling system to promote public health.

The consultation was done by the govt and the FSA is also part of govt, so I wonder if it is biased, e.g. whether the CC system is biased in favour of dairy farming, which I know is big business in the UK. How many different sectors were involved in the consultation? Were more objective external experts involved in making recommendations?

I'm going to read the report in detail because I think I will use it as a key source for my essay. I have also found some non-govt manufacturer reports to use in my essay that give a different viewpoint.

My essay title asks me to look at what steps are being taken now by the govt, and I have other sources that discuss how successful (or not) the front of pack (FoP) labelling system has been and how it is working now. However, this report was a key document when the FoP system started in 2013, which is why it is important to use, even though it is now quite old.

Extract 1

5. Conclusions and Next Steps

5.1 We welcome the responses to the FoP [front of pack] nutrition labelling consultation from a wide range of interested parties and the willingness of many organisations to work with us to achieve greater consistency for future UK FoP labelling.

5.2 Respondents have confirmed to us the importance of FoP labelling, and the need to ensure that any scheme UK Health Ministers might recommend will be one that is consistent across the food products that consumers buy and as widely applied as possible.

5.3 A range of views was expressed on the preferred format, with support for various combinations of %GDAs [guideline daily amounts], colour coding and HML text. However, post consultation, the UK's major food retailers coalesced around a hybrid scheme that includes %GDA and colour coding. An issue on which there was consensus was the need to include information on energy, fat, saturated fats, sugars and salt wherever possible. Whilst it was agreed that labelling would be most useful on composite foods, there was no consensus on the foods that should not carry FoP labelling. We therefore believe that decisions on exemptions should be made by food businesses, with the caveat that they should not set out to be misleading where they are made. In addition, given the responses to the consultation, we will work towards recommending labelling on a 'per portion' basis, and will look further at the possibility of bringing more consistency to when nutrition declarations are given 'as sold' or 'as consumed'.

5.4 Whilst it was clear that the positioning of FoP information can help consumers, prescribing a common position would not work on all packaging/product types.

5.5 There was no call for the development of a common logo and little support for guidance on the highlighting of information on energy content or other information in the form of 'pings'. Therefore, we do not intend to deliberate further on these issues.

Extract from: Food Standards Agency (2013) *Front of pack food labelling: joint response to consultation*, p. 30.

Use the text's organisation

Use the clues given by how the text is organised and what the author is doing in different sections. Don't just glance over headings and subheadings – read them carefully (looking up any words you don't know) and reflect on what they mean and what they say about the author's message. If the text has numbered sections (e.g. 5.1, 5.2), notice how these have been used to group ideas. Next, read the introduction, the first sentence of each paragraph, and then the conclusion. By the time you have done all of this, you will have a pretty good idea of what the text says, giving you a solid platform from which to read the whole text in more detail.

Be clear about what the text is doing overall

The title, headings and introductory section of a text should give you a good idea of its overall purpose. Notice also the phrases used in the abstract of a journal article or the executive summary of a report. If these use words such as 'argue', imply', 'assert' or 'suggests', then the text is likely to be presenting an argument. The executive summary of the 2013 report on food labelling states that 'This is the response to a joint consultation between … ', so we know that the Food Standard Agency's overall aim is to give the findings of the consultation and to say what it thinks about them and what action it intends to take.

… and on what different parts of it are doing

Look at what the author is doing in different parts of the text – you need to distinguish between description, explanation, examples, argument and opinion. Below is a reminder of the difference between these actions, using examples from the FSA 2013 report.

- **Description:** Describes something but does *not* give reasons and does *not* try to judge or persuade the reader of something.

For example:

> Respondents have confirmed to us the importance of FoP labelling, and the need to ensure that any scheme UK Health Ministers might recommend will be one that is consistent across the food products that consumers buy and as widely applied as possible.

- **Explanation:** *Does* give reasons for something (and may also give a conclusion) but does *not* try to judge or persuade the reader of something.

For example:

> There was no call for the development of a common logo and little support for guidance on the highlighting of information on energy content or other information in the form of 'pings'. Therefore, we do not intend to deliberate further on these issues.

- **Argument:** An argument proposes a statement *and* gives reasons and evidence that lead to a particular conclusion *and* uses these reasons and conclusion to persuade the reader of a particular idea or action.

For example:

> A range of views was expressed on the preferred format … Whilst it was agreed that labelling would be most useful on composite foods, there was no consensus on the foods that should *not* carry FoP labelling. We therefore believe that decisions on exemptions should be made by food businesses, with the caveat that they should not set out to be misleading where they are made.

- **Opinion, agreement and disagreement:** These are points of view (perhaps but not necessarily trying to persuade) *without* supporting evidence or logical reasoning. Opinion and dis/agreement are *not* valid arguments and in an academic text should only be given in addition to a properly supported argument, not instead of one.

An example of an opinion would be: '*We think that consumers would prefer labelling on the back of packets rather than on the front.*' (NB. This example is not taken from the FSA report.)

Don't get distracted from the main message

Use your knowledge of the difference between the functions outlined above to identify the main points and argument (also read the sentence before and after key points to make sure you understand their context). Don't get distracted by more minor points or mistake examples for points. Visuals such as 'special facts' boxes might make a text look more interesting but these facts are 'extras' rather than the argument itself.

Use clues given in the language

Read Extract 2 below from an article by Oswald (1997). A student selected this text for the assignment on the links between a society's economic performance and levels of happiness (see p. 65). The numbered annotations to the right of the extract highlight words and phrases that are important in understanding the text. On p. 69 is a summary of what the numbered annotations illustrate.

Extract 2

Happiness and Economic Performance Author: Andrew J. Oswald (1997)

Source: *The Economic Journal*, 107(445): 1815–31. Published by Blackwell Publishing for the Royal Economic Society Stable, pp. 1820–22.

The British Household Panel Survey data show that income has no strong role to play, [in individual well-being] but that joblessness does. Clark and Oswald (1994) fail to find any statistically significant effect from income. The sharp impact of unemployment, however, is illustrated by … data on 6,000 British workers in 1991. Mental distress is twice as high among the unemployed as among those who have work. Interestingly, research suggests that the worst thing about losing one's job is not the drop in take-home income. It is the non-pecuniary distress. To put this differently, most regression results imply that an enormous amount of extra income would be required to compensate people for having no work.

(1) 'Negative' words that are important for understanding Oswald's argument.

(2) Emphasises the contrast between the point made in this sentence and the previous one.

(3) Word to look up now.

(4) Rephrasing a point.

(5) Word to look up later.

Table 5 *The Microeconomics of Happiness in Europe: 1975–86*

	All	Unemployed
Very happy (%)	23.4	15.9
Pretty happy (%)	57.9	51.1
Not too happy (%)	18.6	33.0
	Lowest income quartile people	**Highest-income quartile people**
Very happy (%)	18.8	28.4
Pretty happy (%)	54.5	58.5
Not too happy (%)	26.7	13.1

Source: Di Tella et al. (1996) using Eurobarometer data. Total sample 108,802 observations.

(6) All people in the sample of 108,802 compared with only the unemployed people in the same sample.

(7) Less than a fifth of the whole sample were 'not too happy' but just under a third of the unemployed people in the sample were 'not too happy'.

(7) Double the number of people on low income were 'not too happy' compared to the people on a high income.

(8) Data is from Di Tella et al. 1996 - find this source if possible to check that Oswald has reported it correctly. Also, note that the research was conducted over 25 years ago.

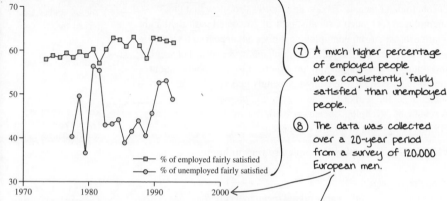

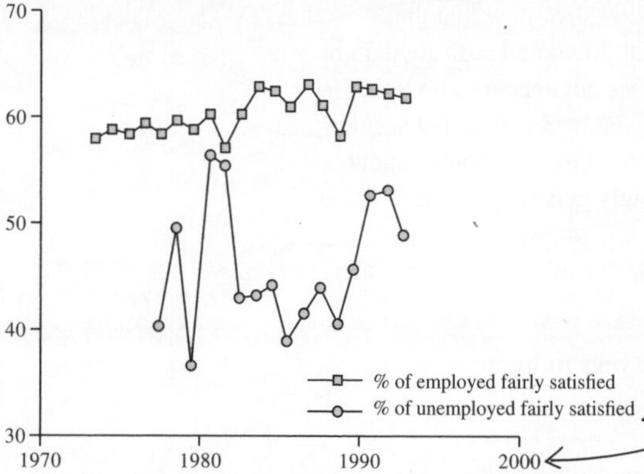

(7) A much higher percentage of employed people were consistently 'fairly satisfied' than unemployed people.

(8) The data was collected over a 20-year period from a survey of 120,000 European men.

Fig. 1 Life-satisfaction levels of the employed and the unemployed: the European countries 1970s–1990s. *Notes.* The vertical axis measures the proportion of people saying they were 'fairly satisfied with life' as a whole. The data source is the Eurobarometer Surveys, which provide a random sample here of approximately 120,000 European men. Running a trend line through each series produces almost exactly the same gradient, namely, just over 0.2.

Eurobarometer data, in Table 5 and Fig. 1, also show that the unemployed feel much less satisfied with life,6 and indicate that the relative distress from unemployment does not appear to be trending downwards through the years (the 'unhappiness gap' is not secularly shrinking). In passing this might be thought to raise doubts about the oft-expressed view that an increasingly generous welfare state is somehow at the root of Europe's economic problems.

A review of psychologists' earlier work is available in Warr et al. (1988). The upshot of all this evidence is:

FINDING 3. Unemployed people are very unhappy.

(9) These verbs link to 'data'.

(10) Indicates a side point.

(11) Refers to the fact that the 'unhappiness gap' is not shrinking.

(Conclusion page 1828)

The conclusions of the paper do not mean that economic forces have little impact on people's lives. A consistent theme through the paper's different forms of evidence has been the vulnerability of human beings to joblessness. Unemployment appears to be the ordinary economic source of unhappiness. If so, economic growth should not be a government's primary concern.

(12) Important word for understanding the context of the argument accurately.

Summary of annotations

(1) Positive or negative words that are important for understanding the author's argument (2) Linking/contrasting words (3) Words you need to know to understand the text (4) Phrases that indicate rephrasing of a point (5) Words you can look up after reading (6) Data – what is measured	(7) Data – what is shown – key statistics (8) Data – who collected it, when and where (9) Understanding what verbs in the sentence refer to (10) Phrases that indicate *minor* points (11) Checking what words such as *this/ that* refer to (12) Words that are important for accurate understanding of the argument

Three useful types of language clue

1 Look out for language 'signposts', which tell you that a main point is coming up (NB: Oswald does not use many such signposts as his writing style is very direct).

For example:

There are three main problems … First … second … finally …
The question/issue/point is …
The main cause/effect/result/implication/flaw is …

Importantly …

My argument is that …

The conclusion is …

The author might also use language signposts to indicate that they are repeating or rephrasing an important point. For example: *to put this differently*, *in other words*, *so*, *another way of saying this is …*

2 The verbs the author uses will tell you what they are doing, so make sure you understand what they mean. Verbs commonly used in academic writing include:

Challenge, claim, demonstrate, dispute, establish, fail, illustrate, indicate
Propose, imply, prove, query, question, reject, show, suggest.

3 Be aware of how authors use words such as *may, might, possibly, tends to* to indicate how sure they are about their claim or the strength of a correlation:

For example:

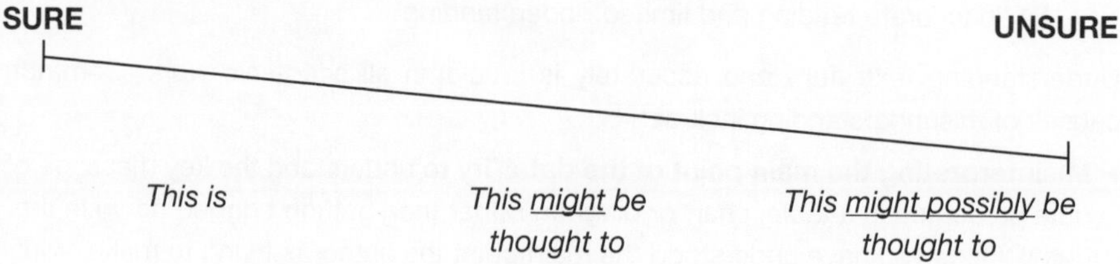

Make sure you have understood *accurately*

- ☑ 'an accurate and critically reflective treatment of all the main issues'
- ☑ 'sources used accurately and concisely'
- ☒ 'inaccurate reading and limited understanding'

Understanding texts fully and accurately is crucial in all academic work. Common causes of misunderstanding include:

- **Misinterpreting the main point of the data:** Try to understand the key message of data presented in a table, chart or diagram rather than getting bogged down in the detail. Once you have understood the main point the author is trying to make, you can go back and analyse the data more closely.
- **Misinterpreting or not noticing comparatives or superlatives:** Words such as *better/the best/worse/the worst/greater/the greatest.* For example, Oswald says that stress is *the worst* thing about being unemployed.
- **Not accurately understanding the degree of something:** For example, Oswald does not state that unemployed people are less satisfied with life but that they are *much less* satisfied. Similarly, Oswald does not say how much economic forces impact on happiness, just that they do have an effect.

- **Overlooking the words *not* or *no* or equivalents:** Pay careful attention to *not*, *no* and other phrases that indicate a negative – mistakes here could mean that you accidentally reverse the author's meaning. Examples of important negatives in Oswald's article are:

  'Clark and Oswald (1994) *fail to* find ... '

  'The conclusions of this paper do *not* mean that economic forces ... '

- **Misinterpreting who says what:** For example, it is not Oswald who states that income does not significantly affect happiness, but Clark and Oswald.

If you are not sure whether you have understood a text accurately, discuss it with other students and/or your tutor, bearing in mind that there might not be one 'correct' interpretation with which everyone agrees.

11 What to do if you get stuck

Myth #7 Intelligent people understand a text straight away.

Difficult text? Feeling confused?

Some academic texts can be difficult because they are overly dense or formal and/or poorly written. If you feel that you are not a great reader, it's probably because you lack subject knowledge and/or good reading strategies rather than intelligence. Reading involves great mental effort, and feeling a bit nervous and confused can, in fact, be a sign that your brain is absorbing, learning and connecting the new information with the old – a good and normal process. Here are some things you can do if you are struggling with a text:

- Remind yourself that you are not alone in feeling confused (most students do at some point) and that things will get easier as you become more familiar with your discipline.
- Stop reading and brainstorm the topic (you could make a mind map) to reactivate the relevant 'knowledge scaffold' in your brain.
- Remind yourself *why* you want to read the text, as this will help you to focus and increase your motivation.
- Find definitions of the key terms and make sure you understand them fully before reading the text.
- Read a section at a time, writing a one-sentence summary of each one before moving on to the next. This will give your brain time to assimilate the new information.
- Read just the headings, introduction and conclusion sections and then go back and read the whole text to the end – things will usually become clearer as you read it through. If you still don't understand the text, find a simpler one on the same topic (or even read the relevant Wikipedia entry) and get a more basic understanding of the topic before going back to the difficult text.
- Discuss the text with other students on your course and/or ask your tutor for advice.

Dealing with difficult words

Myth #5 As you read, you should look up all the words you don't understand.

Don't look up every unknown word as you read – this will slow you down and break your concentration. Use the title, abstract, headings and introduction sections to find key words and look these up *before* reading the whole text. Then, as you read, underline others to look up later. There is no quick, magic solution for developing your word knowledge, but there are things you can do to speed up your academic vocabulary development:

- Look up and practise using the words and phrases you keep coming across in your course and your reading material.
- Use a good English dictionary and 'academic vocabulary' resources that give you not only word definitions but also example sentences and grammatical information.

See *The Student Phrase Book: Vocabulary for Writing at University* in this series.

Dealing with difficult sentences

Here are some tips for unpacking a difficult sentence:

1 Read the sentences before and after the problematic one in order to get a clearer understanding of the context and the message.

2 Break the sentence down into its separate parts. Sentences are usually divided by commas, semi-colons, or words such as: *and*, *or*, *but*, *although*, *which*, *that*, *such as*.

For example, the sentence:

Academic texts should be written in a clear style, although you will often come across complex sentences that have several different parts, such as this one.

can be broken down into four parts:

Academic texts should be written in a clear style

although you will often come across complex sentences

that have several different parts

such as this one.

3 Check that you are clear on the meaning of words that link sentences or parts of a sentence, such as: *however*, *nevertheless*, *despite*, *although*, *whereas*, *moreover*, *also, in addition.*

4 Identify what the pronouns (e.g. *these*, *they*, *this*, *this one*, *which*, *that*, *such*) are referring to.

5 Write out the sentence in your own words using simple vocabulary.

12 Make up your own mind

- ✔ 'willingness to engage critically with the literature and ability to go beyond it'
- ✔ 'ability to analyse materials and their implications'
- ✘ 'does not go beyond the assertion of points derived from the literature'

Critical thinking

Myth #6 **You can't disagree with an academic text because you are not an expert.**

Different readers will disagree on the meanings of words in a text and on the importance and implications of its statements, argument and evidence. For example, in the concluding paragraph of the Oswald extract on p. 68, Oswald states that 'unemployed people are very unhappy'. Different readers will disagree on exactly what Oswald means by 'people' and 'unhappy' and on how to measure unhappiness, and therefore on what Oswald is saying exactly. Readers will also disagree on the implications, consequences and needed actions related to Oswald's claim, such as what governments should do to increase levels of happiness. You too can and should interrogate what an author says, even though you are not an expert in the subject. This process of questioning and challenging texts and ideas is called *critical thinking* or *critical analysis.*

See *Getting critical* in this series.

Context is everything

'lack of awareness of the context of the material.'

To read critically you need to be aware of:

1 Your context

You need to have your own position on something before you can analyse and evaluate someone else's. Moreover, in order to know your position and to use it fairly when judging someone's argument, you need to be aware of your individual biases. For example, when reading the Oswald text extract, think about whether you have an underlying belief that wealth *does* make people happy and, if so, whether and how this underlying belief of yours might influence your views on Oswald's argument.

2 The author's context

Authors have their own contexts and biases of course and being aware of these will help you to read the text critically. Find out who the author is/was and who they work/ed for (you can use the 'about us' tabs on websites as well as Google and Wikipedia). Also think about the author's historical, political and social context and what ideological outlooks are reflected in their ideas. Oswald's writing context, for example, includes the fact that he is a highly educated academic whose work includes mathematical models of trade union behaviour.

3 The text's context

Think about when, where, why and for whom the text was written and about how the text connects to other texts and material on the topic. The report on front of pack nutrition labelling on p. 55, for example, was written on behalf of a group of government bodies (including the Food Standards Agency) to report on and respond to their findings of a consultation they conducted with various food industry and retailer organisations and, to a lesser extent, non-industry bodies and individual consumers. The audience for the report was wide-ranging (including all those involved in the consultation) and was the first government agency report to look at the issue of food labelling in the UK.

Identify assumptions, gaps and flaws

As you read, engage the author in a challenging 'conversation':

- What are their assumptions, and do you think they are correct? For example, one underlying assumption in the Oswald text extract on p. 68 is that it is the government's job to decrease unemployment. Do you agree with this assumption?

- How has the data been collected and reported? Could there be other explanations for their correlations and conclusions? If the author has used data from another source, have they used it fairly? For example, Oswald uses data from Di Tella et al. 1996, and so you might want to find this primary source to check that Oswald has used this data in an accurate and balanced manner.
- How has the author used evidence? Do their reasons and conclusion link together logically or are there flaws in the argument? For example, Oswald claims that 'Unemployed people are very unhappy', yet the data on which he bases this claim (Table 5 on p. 66) includes only European men (Fig. 1 on p. 67).
- Does the author use persuasive phrases such as: *surely*, *we have to remember*, *it is perfectly clear that*, *it is obvious that*, *it is a fact that*, *one can't fail to recognise that* without providing evidence to support them?

Stand back and evaluate

Stand back and give the text a final evaluation. What is the way of thinking of the author? What is the text trying to do and how well does it do it? Why do you think people read this text? Do *you* think it is worth reading and if so, why?

Reading and rereading

As mentioned briefly on p. 48, you will usually need to read a text several times in order to understand, analyse and evaluate it properly. You will also need some conscious thinking time and some 'time out' between readings. The gaps are important, as this is when your brain will work in the background to form and separate out your own ideas.

Below is a guide for this rereading process, although in reality your reading and thinking processes won't be as structured or separated as this:

- **1st reading:** get an idea of the text's overall structure and meaning and look up key words.
- **Thinking gap:** reflect briefly on the text structure and general meaning.
- **2nd reading:** get a more detailed and thoughtful understanding of the text.
- **Thinking gap:** form questions and views and summarise the text in your own words.
- **Time out:** (anything from two hours to two days) don't think about the text at all!
- **3rd reading:** analyse and interrogate the text further and identify its strengths and weaknesses.
- **Thinking gap:** evaluate the text from the perspective of your own ideas.

13 Get the wider picture

- ☑ 'detailed *and* broad knowledge base'
- ☑ 'clear understanding of the nature of the material'
- ☑ 'mindful of other interpretations'

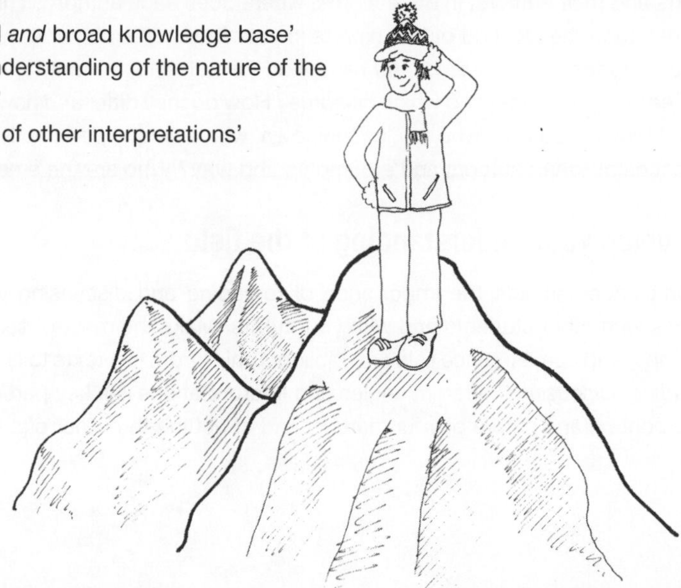

Location, location, location!

As you read more sources, build up a mental picture of the location of the different texts and their authors; in other words, where does each author 'sit' in the subject? To understand the location of the experts in your field, reflect on how each text you read relates to the other material you have read (or will read) on that topic. Which authors agree with each other and which disagree? How do they differ and how are they similar? Are there any authors who are 'on their own' with a unique perspective? Which are the most established authors and arguments and why? Who are the emerging stars?

Develop your understanding of the field

Don't underestimate the importance of rereading and discussing your reading and ideas with other students and with your tutors. Make the most of seminars and study groups, and use reference lists and bibliographies from key texts to find relevant further reading. Discussing different angles and interpretations is a key part of understanding the context and nature of your material and of getting the wider picture.

Summary

- Develop an active, critical approach to texts so that you can reach your own reasoned and unique understanding of them.
- Be clear on the structure of the text, its overall function and the function of its different parts and identify the key points.
- Speed up your word knowledge by noting down, looking up and then using words and phrases that are new to you.
- If you are finding a text difficult, remind yourself that this is normal and then use specific strategies to move forward.
- Reread and have thinking gaps between readings to give your brain time to form its own ideas.
- Develop your knowledge of the wider picture by identifying where the authors in the field sit and what your own position is within it.

PART 5

Making Notes

THE ESSENTIALS

14 Active and purposeful notes

Myth #8 You don't need to make notes, you can just annotate and copy and paste.

Although this book is separated into 'reading' and 'note-making' sections, in reality, these two processes are an integrated, back-and-forth process. We looked briefly at active note-making in Chapters 1 and 2, and two points to remember are that you should decide *why* you want to make notes before you start making them, and that you should use notes as an aid to your *thinking* process. You should make notes to help you understand a text and also as a 'springboard' or reflective tool for engaging at a deeper level with your subject.

Making notes can:

- help you to concentrate on what you are reading
- keep you motivated by tracking and signalling your progress
- help you remember information more easily
- start you on the process of using your own words and style
- give you your own unique record of the text
- help you to reflect and make connections between different pieces of knowledge
- lead to a better understanding of your subject
- and, because of the above, probably result in higher marks.

Below are three lists of some of the things you can make notes on before, during and/or after reading, depending on your reading and note-making purpose.

***Before* you start reading, you can note down:**

- random, creative thoughts and ideas on the topic
- what you already know about the topic
- what your views are on the topic or issue
- what you know about other sources and texts that discuss the topic
- predictive questions on what the text might say.

***During* and/or *after* reading, you can note down:**

- a record of your own understanding of the text structure (and argument)
- a record of your understanding of the text's key points
- points and ideas that address your own angle, question or argument
- ideas for your own project or research
- words or phrases to look up later
- the reference details of sources mentioned in the text or in the end bibliography
- questions, things to investigate or discuss with colleagues or tutors
- random, creative thoughts and ideas on the topic.

***After* reading, you can note down:**

- your own summary and reflection (in your own words) of the key points in the text
- the information in different organisational patterns to reveal different connections and help form your own ideas
- your own thoughts and arguments on the issue
- your ideas on whether/how points from the text relate to those of other sources
- your more personal feelings on the text and topic.

Don't take notes, make notes

Myth #9 **Effective notes have all the points from the text copied down.**

Unless you are trying to learn something by heart, there isn't much point in copying down lots of individual sentences or chunks from the text – it is a waste of time and usually means that you are on 'autopilot' rather than actively reading and thinking. Instead, your notes should 'tell the story' of the text from the perspective of your own reading purpose and questions. Your notes should clearly show the text's overall structure, hierarchy and main points, expressed mainly in your own words. Understanding the main thread of the text will enable you to recall smaller details later if you need to.

Read first, note later

Try reading the text without making any notes and focus on understanding and thinking. Then summarise the text's main message in your mind or out loud, and make written notes from memory, going back to the text only if you need to check something. Finally, write your own simple summary of the text's key points in your own words.

Write short summary comments

After reading and making notes on each main section of the text, use your notes to write a short summary. Your choice of verbs should reflect accurately what the author does in that section; for example, a summary of Extract 1 on p. 59 might include the sentence: 'The report *states* that respondents want a food labelling system but *proposes* that the exemptions to such a system are decided by the food manufacturers.'

15 Key features of effective notes

You can make notes in any form that works for you, but make sure that they:

- have a purpose and achieve this purpose (see Chapter 14)
- give you a clear picture of the structure of the argument or points in the text
- show the difference between main and minor points
- show the difference between arguments and the evidence or examples used to support them
- make clear the difference between the author's words and ideas and your own
- make sense to you weeks or months (or even years) after writing them.

After reading Extract 2 on p. 65, a student made a page of notes that do everything listed above; read them and see if you agree.

Oswald AJ (1997) Happiness and economic performance. *The Economic Journal*, 107(445): 1815–31. Found from Infolinx → ejournals → JSTOR. Notes – pp 1815 & 1828. Made on 17/05/2022

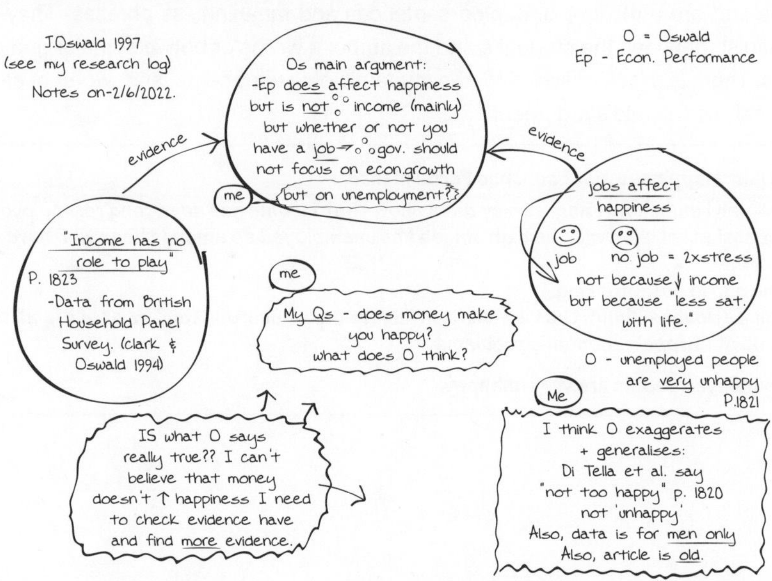

J.Oswald 1997
(see my research log)
Notes on-2/6/2022.
O = Oswald
Ep - Econ. Performance
Os main argument:
-Ep does affect happiness but is not income (mainly) but whether or not you have a job → gov. should not focus on econ.growth
me
but on unemployment?
evidence
evidence
"Income has no role to play"
P. 1823
-Data from British Household Panel Survey. (clark & Oswald 1994)
jobs affect happiness
job
no job = 2xstress
not because ↓ income but because "less sat. with life."
O - unemployed people are very unhappy
P.1821
me
My Qs - does money make you happy?
what does O think?
IS what O says really true?? I can't believe that money doesn't ↑ happiness I need to check evidence have and find more evidence.
Me
I think O exaggerates + generalises:
Di Tella et al. say "not too happy" p. 1820
not 'unhappy'
Also, data is for men only
Also, article is old.

An example of ineffective notes

Now look at the ineffective notes below. These notes don't have adequate reference details and are a mixture of copied sentences and meaningless phrases. They don't distinguish between the student's and the author's words or between major and minor points. There is a lack of space for the student's own comments, and, worst of all, they do not show Oswald's argument.

> Oswald. **Happiness and Economic Performance.**
>
> - British Household Panel survey data show that income has no strong role to play.
> - mental stress is twice as high among the unemployed as among those who have work.
> - the gap is not shrinking.
> - raises doubts about the view that an increasingly generous welfare state is at the root of Europe's economic problems.
>
> **Unemployed people are very unhappy.**

Effective notes

Below, in a bit more detail, is a list of the key features of effective notes and comments on why they are important.

Key features	Why?
Full reference details, including page numbers	So that you can reference the source in your assignments and can find it again if you need to.
Information on when/where you made the notes	To help you remember and trace your research process.
Your reading and note-making purpose and questions	To keep you focused and therefore less prone to copying down too much from the text. If you need to go back for more information later, you can but you probably won't need to.
Information that is not too detailed or too brief	Your notes should be brief but also need to make sense to you, so avoid writing down lots of 'unattached' single words.

Key features	Why?
A clear distinction between the main points, minor points, evidence and examples	So that you have a clear understanding and record of the main argument (think about whether you even need to make notes on minor points). If you can't separate out the main points in a text, you probably don't understand it and need to read it again.
A clear system for distinguishing between: **quotation** **close paraphrase (where you have used a few of your own words)** **and** **paraphrase (where you have used mostly/all your own words)**	To avoid accidental plagiarism when using source material in your assignment. Use quotation marks to remind yourself that you have copied from the text. If you paraphrase closely, you should also record this, as you will need to re-express the idea in your own words if you want to use it as acceptable paraphrase in your assignment. Try to use your own words as much as possible in your notes. You may be worried about changing the meaning of the text or feel that you can't put things into your own words as well as the original, but your confidence will increase with practice.

Key features	Why?
A clear system for distinguishing between the author's ideas and comments and your own	To avoid accidental plagiarism by confusing the author's ideas with your own. Use shapes, colours, fonts or separate spaces – anything, as long as it will be clear to you when you go back to your notes which comments and ideas are yours.
A key to abbreviations	So that when you read your notes at a later date, you will know what your abbreviations mean.
White space	In case you need to add anything later.
Use separate pages for different sections and/or sources and/or write on only one side of paper	So that you can rearrange sections and pages later if you want to.
Numbered pages	So that if your notes get jumbled, you can put them back in their correct order.

Below is a second example of effective notes, this time on Extract 1 on p. 59. The student read the text and then noted down the key points from memory. They then reread the text and added a few more details to their notes. Notice that the student has not copied down any quotations but has mainly used their own words. Where they have closely paraphrased the text, they have put [CP]. They have put the key points of the argument in bold and used a separate column for their own comments and thoughts. Finally, the student has written their own summary and reflection on the article.

1 Food Standards Agency (2013) *Front of pack nutrition labelling: joint response to consultation* Policy paper by Department of Health and others. www.gov.uk/government/publications/response-to-consultation-on-front-of-pack-nutrition-labelling-2 Accessed, read and notes made on 13/06/2022. Found by searching on the FSA homepage.
My purpose and Qs: *To find out what govt is doing re food labelling and health (esp. coronary heart disease = CHD) and to see if the report has any critical evaluation or comments from the people it consulted.* My prediction – this govt report will be biased towards the food industry who I guess won't want food labelling (FL) on unhealthy foods as this might reduce sales.

My comments/questions	Notes on text
	p. 30 of the article:
What does 'wide range' mean? Me to look at back of report to find out who was consulted. What does this comb. mean in practice? Won't it be confusing?	A wide range of groups consulted. Respnds want a 'consistent and widely applicable' scheme. Majority view was for scheme that combines guideline daily amount (GDA)% with colour coding and high/med/low info. [CP]
! this contradicts the idea of consistency*. This seems to me to be a fudge in favour of the manufs. Who decides 'misleading'?	Respnds wanted labelling for 'composite foods' but couldn't agree on what should <u>not</u> be labelled. So: Report recs. That food industry should decide, as long as FL not misleading.
Was this done? Me to research what happened 2013 to now.	Report says having info in same position on all packaging won't work. NO support for common logos or catch phrases. Promised action – consistent scheme combining %GDAs and colour coding by April 2013.

My own summary and viewpoint

The report states that respondents want a food labelling system but proposes that the exemptions to such a system are decided by the food manufacturers.

This Dept of Health report showed progress on food labelling and a specific target for Spring 2013 to bring my country (UK) in line with EU regulations on clear food labelling.

However, I think that using a combination of %GDA and colour coding is unnecessarily and purposely confusing for consumers (previous report Lobstein et al. 2009 showed that consumers prefer the 'traffic lights' system).

Also, allowing the food industry to choose when and when not to label foods definitely seems to me to have been a cynical attempt to favour sales over consumers' health.

Summary

- Making notes can help you to develop your own ideas and express them in your own way.
- Have a purposeful 'before, during and after' approach to note-making.
- Try reading and thinking first and then making some notes afterwards.
- Your notes should record clearly your understanding of the main points and how you see the relationships between the ideas in the text.
- Your notes don't have to be neat but you do need to be able to understand them when you read them back in the months or years ahead.
- Your notes reflect your own understanding, form of expression and ideas on the text and so are unique to you.

PART 6

DECIDE *HOW* YOU WILL MAKE NOTES

16 Different note-making formats

Myth #10 Making notes in lines and columns is the best technique.

You probably already have your own way of making notes but experimenting with a format you don't usually use might help you to arrive at new ways of understanding and thinking. For example, if you usually make pattern notes from a text but find that you sometimes lose the structure of the author's ideas, you might want to try making some linear notes. Conversely, if you usually use a linear style, try making pattern notes (e.g. a spidergram) for a change to see if doing so helps you make more creative connections between ideas in the text.

Importantly, however you make notes, they should have the essential features listed on p. 97, such as a having a record of the source details and whether you are quoting, paraphrasing or writing down a comment of your own.

Voice recordings

- **Pros:** good for expressing your questions and thoughts on a text while you are reading it and for recording your own spoken summary. Voice notes help you develop your own understanding and use of your own words and style. They also help reduce copying from the text and making too many notes, and, of course, you can't cut and paste.
- **Cons:** you don't have a written record unless you use speech-to-text software, but this only transcribes in a basic 'sentence' format and can't create notes that show structure, groupings and connections between ideas.
- **Tip:** voice record your ideas as you read a text, then use these voice notes as a springboard for your questions as you read the text a second time and make notes in written form.

Annotations

- **Pros:** good for producing a visual picture of the structure of a text if you highlight and annotate main points. Annotations are attached to the text and so you can refer directly from one to the other.

- **Cons:** there is usually only space to write short annotations, even when using annotation software. Making annotations also tends to bypass the process of writing down your own understanding of the text in your own words.
- **Tips:**

  Go easy on the highlighter

  You might not have a clear idea of what the key points in a text are until you have read to the end, so to avoid being stuck with highlighting you want to change and instead use pencil lines down the margin that can be rubbed out. A better use of the highlighter is for emphasising key points when you review your notes.

  Explain your reactions to yourself

  It's good to react to the text, but don't just put **!!** or **?** in the margin; note down your reaction in words.

  Don't just annotate

  Use a combination of annotation and separate written notes that record your thoughts, questions and interpretation of the text.

Linear or 'list' notes

Linear notes are those written in a structured 'down the page' way, often using lists, bullet points and/or numbering.

- **Pros:** easy format to type and good for distinguishing between major and minor points and examples.
- **Cons:** encourage copying of structure and words from the text and can lead to writing down too much information. Not good for seeing connections between ideas in the text.
- **Tip:** start each new point on a new line and use indentation and/or spacing to show how information groups together. Leave white space where possible and try to produce clear notes that are not too detailed or dense.

Cornell or 'split page' notes

These are linear style notes that also have a separate column for your own comments and a space at the end for your own summary. The notes on p. 101 are an example of split page notes.

- **Pros:** you have a clear separation of your own ideas and also your own summary.
- **Cons**: not great for creative interpretation or for making connections between ideas.

- **Tip:** as with all note formats, don't write down too much detail – make your notes as clear and as spaced as possible.

Paragraph notes

This is when you read (or listen) without making notes and write your own summary afterwards in the form of a paragraph.

- **Pros:** good for helping you to process and understand the text in your own way and for summarising it in your own words.
- **Cons:** you might not be able to remember details or large amounts of information (but, as we have said, this is usually a good thing).
- **Tip:** don't forget to write down the source details and relevant page numbers. Also, keep track of words or phrases taken directly from the text. Finally, summarise only what is in the text, using a separate paragraph for your own comments.

Table notes

This is when you make notes in columns under headings, as in this example.

Different theories of job satisfaction

Affect	Dispositional	Equity	Discrepancy	2 factor	Job characteristics
Edwin A. Locke. Most famous theory ...	Judge, Locke, Durham, Staw. Innate dispositions that ...	Idea that people are concerned mainly with ...			

- **Pros**: good for comparing different strands, different authors' ideas or different possible viewpoints on a topic, and/or for noting down the advantages and disadvantages of something.
- **Cons:** don't allow you to create your own groupings or connections.
- **Tip:** you can use tables to prepare a generalised note-making framework or template for any text or lecture.

Pattern notes

'Pattern' or 'visual' notes is a broad term that includes the use of drawings, spider diagrams (also called 'mind maps') and flow method notes.

- **Pros:** allow you to record the overall structure of someone's argument in a creative way, making connections and revealing relationships between ideas in the text. Pattern notes also help limit copying down or writing too many notes. An example of pattern notes is on p. 114.
- **Cons:** less easy to record clearly the structure and hierarchies of the ideas in the text.
- **Tips:** use numbering, colours or symbols to record the structure of the text and to distinguish between your ideas and the author's. If you are using paper, use landscape and/or large unlined sheets and experiment with coloured paper.

Spatial notes

This term is used by Lia (2020) to describe notes in which points and ideas are grouped using the space on the paper.

For example:

> Neural Networks for handwritten doc. Recognition. p.4564
>
> Features of handwriting.
> irreg. shapes and styles
> characters not always clear or finished
> sometimes written on rough surfaces
>
> Network processing probs:
> Puts characts. in wrong category
> Unable to recgn. all characts.

- **Pros:** help record a clear structure and hierarchy (as in linear notes) and also encourages the use of space to reflect creative groupings rather than just repeating the structure of the text.
- **Cons:** not as good as pattern notes for making connections *between* groupings.
- **Tip:** don't feel you have to use a particular special structure – write anywhere you like on the paper to represent how you think different points group together.

Spider diagrams

Spider diagrams (sometimes called 'nuclear notes') are a type of pattern notes in which you start from a central point and then note down subpoints and connections that stem from this nucleus. The pattern notes on p. 114 are in spidergram form. The pros, cons and tips for spider diagrams are similar to those for pattern notes, as given on the previous page.

Mind maps

Another term for a spidergram is a 'mind map', but as the name implies, a mind map is not really a way of making notes *on* a text but of brainstorming your knowledge and ideas *before* you read. Mind maps are also good for brainstorming your ideas on an assignment topic.

Below is an example of a mind map a student made for their essay on lifestyle-related diseases on p. 12.

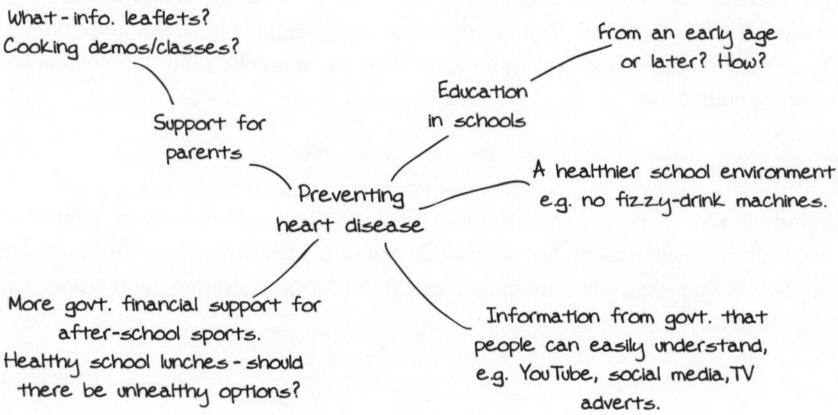

What - info. leaflets?
Cooking demos/classes?
Support for parents
From an early age or later? How?
Education in schools
A healthier school environment e.g. no fizzy-drink machines.
Preventing heart disease
More govt. financial support for after-school sports.
Healthy school lunches - should there be unhealthy options?
Information from govt. that people can easily understand, e.g. YouTube, social media, TV adverts.

17 Making notes in lectures and seminars

Making notes in lectures

Lectures can be hard to understand due to a combination of unfamiliar vocabulary, speaker style or accent and the fact that you can't control the speaker's speed or put them on repeat. To get the most from your lectures and seminars, try to develop a 'before, during and after' approach, just as you would for a written text you want to read. You will see from the list below that most of the physical note-making work should be done before and after the lecture or seminar rather than during it. This approach is equally useful for both live and recorded lectures – it will help you understand a recorded talk in one or two viewings rather than having to listen to it multiple times.

Before the lecture

- Do any required reading preparation.
- Read the lecture title, handouts and slides if available, and use the main headings to prepare a note-making template. At the top, put your own questions and thoughts on the topic to help you keep your notes focussed.

- Check both the meaning and pronunciation of key terms.
- Brainstorm what you know about the topic.
- If you haven't heard the speaker before, see if you can find a recording of them on your university website or YouTube in order to familiarise yourself with their style of speech and delivery.
- Check the module website the day before the lecture for any last-minute changes or information.

During the lecture

- Sit towards the front of the lecture room if you can – it's easy to become distracted and disengaged when sitting at the back.
- If the lecturer gives a handout at the start of a face-to-face lecture, *don't* try to read it while the lecturer is speaking; read it afterwards.
- Listen, try to understand and engage rather than make lots of notes.
- Use your prepared template to write brief notes, thoughts, questions and things to look up later.
- You can also use what is sometimes called 'the flow method' of making notes, which is when you listen and engage and just make brief notes that represent the

main points of 'the story'. The idea is to get a good understanding of the story/ argument *as* you listen, rather than making lots of notes that you have to read after the lecture in order to understand it.

Things to listen out for:

- The start of the lecture when the speaker usually outlines the structure of the lecture and states key points.
- The end of the lecture when the speaker usually summarises the most important points covered.
- The lecturer raising their voice and/or speaking more slowly to emphasise key points.
- Whether the lecturer is giving a key point, a fact, a description, an explanation, an example or an opinion.
- Words that qualify a statement (e.g. *always*, *rarely*) or words that give a negative, such as *no, not, never, fails to* or *neglects to.*
- 'Signposting language' that will help you understand the structure, direction and key points of the lecture.

  Examples of signposting language are:

Structure and logical sequence:

first, second, third, next, then, there are (three) main factors, consequently, because of this, for this reason, as a result, this is due to, therefore, one effect is

Cue words for important points:

Crucially, importantly, remember, especially, obviously, as I said before

Words that qualify a statement:

always, sometimes, usually, generally, rarely, never, only

Cue words for a change in direction or contrast:

in contrast, on the other hand, a different, but, however, although

Words that indicate examples or supporting evidence:

such as, for example, for instance, an illustration of this is, research/a study by X shows that, evidence from Y shows that

After the lecture

- Review, amend and add to any notes you made. Add things such as date and time and a key to any abbreviations you used. Check that you can see which information is from the lecturer and which are your own comments. Underline key points, correct any errors and look up any words or terms you don't understand.
- Critically review the lecture and material. Write down your own summary, evaluation and ideas. What follow-up questions would you like to ask, perhaps in your next seminar? What further research and references do you want to chase up? How does the content relate to the rest of the module and your course in general? What was said in the lecture that really interested you and why?

Making notes in seminars

The 'before, during and after' strategies given above for making notes in lectures also apply to seminars, except that during a seminar you will probably take even fewer notes. In a seminar, you are an active participant in the discussion, so listen, think and contribute, making only brief notes on your thoughts and questions in preparation for something *you* want to say.

Try it out for yourself

Try out some of the strategies and tips given in this chapter by watching part or all of an online lecture or podcast from an open courseware site. Good sites for these are:

www.academicearth.org
www.TED.com
www.khanacademy.org
www.Utubersity.com
www.openculture.com
www.freevideolectures.com
www.learnerstv.com

18 Tools and technology

Many students use a mixture of digital and paper mediums to make notes. The most important thing is the quality of thought you gain through making them, whatever medium you use. However, the type of tools you use can have an impact on your thinking, so it can be useful to use different things at different thinking stages. You could also try handwriting notes if you always type, or note-making software if you always use paper, to see whether using a different medium contributes to your creative process.

Below are brief descriptions of different note-making tools and technology and the main advantages and disadvantages of each one.

Pen and paper

- **Pros:** relatively cheap, portable, do not need power and are unlikely to be stolen. In addition, you can spread papers out on a table or floor and get creative by arranging and rearranging them in different ways to help you see different patterns and connections. Although you can move digital documents around on a screen, it is harder to do so while also keeping track of your notes as a whole, even when using a large screen or two screens. (You can, of course, print out your typewritten notes and then move them around on the floor.)

- You can't be tempted to copy and paste from the text. This is an advantage if you have a tendency to do this too much rather than make effective, critical notes.
- Pen and paper are particularly good for making creative spider diagrams and mind maps due to the quick and free-flowing nature of this medium.
- **Cons:** you have to buy the pens and paper and keep them somewhere. You can't save, share, copy, import, export or manipulate using note-making software.
- **Tip:** if you are use A4 pages, buy the kind with holes so that you can put them into a file or folder. For making creative pattern notes using paper, see the tips on p. 111.

Notebooks and journals

- **Pros:** useful to carry around, and they keep your notes together in one place.
- **Cons:** you can't reorder the pages unless you use only one side of the pages and then cut or tear them out.
- **Tip:** put your name and a safe form of contact details on the inside cover.

Index or note cards

These are small cards of stiff paper used to record a single idea, theme or piece of information. They are called 'index cards' because they are often used to store information in a particular order. 'Note cards' is a more general term.

- **Pros:** they encourage you to have only one idea on each card and therefore to stick to the main points (cards are particularly useful for noting key terms and concepts, theories and models). If you tend to make too many notes, you can go through your cards after making your notes and reject cards that are not relevant.
- Cards are particularly good for reviewing, ordering and reordering information to suit different purposes, such as building an essay plan. You can even shuffle the cards and lay them out randomly to encourage new and creative ways of thinking. Cards are also useful for building up an ordered research retrieval system and for reviewing notes generally.
- **Cons:** you are restricted to small amounts of information on each card. They also have the same disadvantages as paper regarding storage, backup and exporting/importing.
- **Tip:** leave a small space at the bottom of each card to add source information, cross-references and your own comments.

Front of card

Oswald AJ (1997) Happiness and economic performance. *The Economic Journal*, 107(445): 1815–31.

Date of notes: 17/05/2022, p. 1827

Evidence that economic progress only marginally affects happiness

Back of card

4 main pieces of evidence:

- Only fractional ↑ in happiness in US since WWII despite ↑↑ wealth
- Europe – only slightly higher levels than 20 yrs ago
- No. of male suicides ↑ in nearly all Western countries since '70s
- In UK and US job satsfctn has <u>not</u> increased (where data is available)

Smart pens

There are different smart (or digital) pens on the market. Here are a few things to consider if you are thinking of buying one.

- **Pros:** combine some of the advantages of handwriting notes with the fact that they are saved directly onto your device or can be uploaded.
- **Cons:** they are expensive and easily lost or stolen. They depend on battery power and can have limited storage space. They can be heavy, particularly if they include a voice recorder. Some smart pens require specialised paper.
- **Tip:** try them out before buying. Check for weight, comfort and feel and check the cost of any add ons such as paper or graphic tablet. Think carefully about how much you will use a smart pen.

Note-making software

Even if you already use note-making software, it's worth going to any workshops your university provides on note-making and reference management software so that you know how to make the most of them. Your library should also be able to help you access more specialised software (sometimes referred to as assistive technology), such as Dragon speech-to-text.

Here are the most commonly used note-making software packages and applications.

Note-making and annotation:

- Microsoft Office 365 OneNote. It has annotation tools.
- Microsoft Office Word annotation function using Review' ➢ 'comments'
- Apple Notes
- Evernote (free, basic version)
- Adobe Acrobat's annotating tools.

Speech to text:

- Microsoft Office 365 OneNote. The 'Learning Tools' ➢ Dictate ➢ 'Voice to Text' function
- Microsoft Office 365. The 'Home' ➢ 'Dictate' function
- Google Docs 'Voice Typing' function
- Apple Dictate. The 'Edit' ➢ 'Start Dictation' function on an Apple Mac
- Audio Notetaker by Sonocent. This works for PCs or Macs. Not free
- Dragon Naturally Speaking. Not free. You need to 'speech train' this software.

Spatial, pattern and visual notes:

- Microsoft Office 365 OneNote Mind mapping function
- Microsoft Visio. For flowcharts and diagrams. Not free
- MindView, XMind, Inspiration and MindManager. All of these software programmes are good for making spider diagrams and mind maps. Not free
- Microsoft Word 'SmartArt' and 'Drawing Tools' functions. This is free but is not very quick or easy to use for making spider diagrams and mind maps.

Citation and reference management software

This type of software is really useful. The three main packages are:

- **OneNote:** You will probably have free access at university to OneNote as part of Microsoft Office, and this note-making software package can also create and manage your references.
- **RefWorks:** Many universities also provide student use of RefWorks, which, as the name suggests, is reference managing software.
- **Mendeley:** Another good free package is Mendeley, which can also function for note-making as well as reference management. You can use this software as a web version or download to your desktop.

Summary

- Effective notes show both the structure and development of the ideas in a text, together with your own insights into the patterns and connections between them.
- Make the most of your lectures and seminars by adopting a 'before, during and after' approach and by listening and engaging when you are in them rather than making lots of notes.
- Experiment with a different note-making format or a combination of formats, to reach deeper and more creative insights.
- The quality of your understanding, engagement and thinking processes reflected in your notes is more important than the medium or tools you use.

PART 7

MAKE THE MOST OF YOUR NOTES

19 Review and rework your notes

Reviewing and reworking your notes is an important part of the critical thinking process and will also help you to use them effectively in your written assignments.

Review your notes

- Read your notes (and add to them if necessary) to check that they make sense to you and give you a clear picture of the structure of the text and the development of the author's information, ideas and argument.
- Check that you have noted the source details and where you found it, and that your notes are dated and have page numbers and an abbreviation key.

Rework your notes. Try doing one or more of the following:

- From your notes, write a summary of the text in your own words (think of what you would say if a friend asked you to summarise what the text says); this will help you clarify your understanding and your ability to express it.
- Rewrite your notes using a different note-making format to reveal patterns or connections you had not previously seen.
- Reorganise your notes around your own unique question or angle, and/or your assignment title, adding comments and identifying any knowledge gaps.
- Review your notes from other texts and lectures on the same topic and look for connections and similarities or differences between different ideas, arguments, evidence and viewpoints.
- Bring together your ideas from your notes on different texts in a written critical summary and/or reflection that expresses your understanding of the various texts you have read.

Using your notes to write a critical reflection

This allows you to restate the author's information and ideas in your own way and to further develop your own questioning and evaluation of them. A written reflection also helps you to relate these ideas to what you already know and to see how they fit into the wider picture of your subject. Finally, a written critical reflection will help you to see why, how and where you want to use these sources in your own assignment, and will allow you to start using your own words and style for when you do.

The style of your reflection can be informal, but it's useful to write in full sentences. Use your own words and phrases as far as possible, and put any exact phrases from the text in quotation marks so that you can keep track of them. Include a short summary of what you have learnt, and if the text has an important data diagram, table or chart, summarise what it shows in one sentence.

Below is an example of a short critical reflection on Oswald's article (see Extract 2 on p. 65) written by a student doing reading for the assignment title on p. 12.

Oswald's main argument is that economic performance *does* affect people's happiness but only really because it influences employment rates. He argues that it is whether people have a job or not that has a significant effect on their well-being, not income. I think that this is a very interesting finding and not one I had expected. I can see how this might be the case, but I think that Oswald is exaggerating his claim. His evidence has some flaws in it and his finding that 'Unemployed people are very unhappy' seems to me to be oversimplified. The data he uses in fact only looks at men and also does not say that people without jobs are *very* unhappy. Also, I know some unemployed people who are very happy!

Still, Oswald is clearly an authority in this field, has published widely and the background notes give details of where I can find more evidence for his claim. I will probably use this article as a main source in my essay as support for my argument that the relationship between economic performance and happiness is extremely complex and so not easy to quantify. First, though, I need to check out more closely some of the data Oswald uses and also try to find other authors that have different perspectives and/or can provide more up to date evidence.

Sharing notes as part of a collaborative assignment

As we saw in Chapters 14 and 15, your notes are a record of your own thoughts, questions and understanding of the text, written in your own way, and so they belong to you. If your course requires you to collaborate with other students and work as a team on a project or assignment, then, of course, you should share and discuss your ideas as you work together to produce the final assignment. However, it is best *not* to give copies of your notes to your team members because this could lead to confusion about who contributed what to the final piece of work.

Accidental collusion

Collusion is when someone uses someone else's work in their own without declaring that they have done so and is therefore a form of cheating. As your notes are unique to you and part of your own scholarship and research, it's best not to lend them to anyone else. To be clear, you *should* discuss with other students the understandings and ideas you have come to while reading and making notes, as this is an important part of being in an academic community, but you should *not* give physical copies of your notes to other students unless required to do.

Accidental plagiarism

When you use your notes to write up your assignment, make sure you give a reference every time you use ideas or information from source material. Importantly, you must do this regardless of whether you have expressed the author's ideas in their words (as quotation) or in your own (as paraphrase). Even when you express the author's ideas completely in your own words, you must give a reference in the body of your assignment and also in the bibliography – failing to do so constitutes plagiarism.

Accidentally misrepresenting an author

Always try to represent and report what an author says in a fair and accurate manner. Be aware of how the author's idea you are discussing fits into their whole argument and present this context clearly. For example, you would be misrepresenting Oswald if you said that he views economic growth as unimportant because, in fact, what he says is that economic growth is not the most important thing (see p. 68).

Don't let your sources take control

Avoid producing a piece of work that consists mainly of large chunks of written-up notes sewn together by only thin threads of your own sentences.

✘

✔

Your argument and *your* voice should stand out and dominate your assignment, and so you need to make your sources and notes work for you in support of *your* answer to the assignment title.

- ☑ 'sources used accurately and concisely but do not dominate'
- ☑ 'evaluates evidence and synthesises materials clearly to develop persuasive arguments'
- ☑ 'evidence used appropriately to support their conclusion'

Summary

- Your notes should give you a clear picture of the structure and development of the ideas in the source and of how you see patterns and connections between them.
- Experiment with different note formats and try using more than one format for different stages of your reading and note-making process.
- Write a short reflection from your notes to consolidate your reading and thinking and to help you to express your ideas in your own way.
- Rework your notes around your own questions and angles and use them to address your assignment title.
- Store your notes in an organised way to keep them safe from physical damage or loss, as you may need them as you progress in your studies and career.
- Your notes are part of your research and the development of your unique understanding, insights and voice in relation to source material – they therefore belong to you.

Final comment

Taking control of your reading and making clear, individual and insightful notes is a skill that takes time to learn, so be patient with yourself – everybody finds this challenging at times. The most important thing is to *engage* with your reading texts, your lectures and your seminars, and to *think* about the ideas contained within them, using the note-making process to help you to do this.

Believe it or not, good academic work involves a lot of creativity, and if you have an active and engaged approach to reading and making notes, you will be surprised at the new and creative ideas you can generate.

Appendix 1: Examples of common abbreviations for note-making

Full word or phrase	Abbreviation or symbol	Full word or phrase	Abbreviation or symbol
and/plus	+	maximum	max.
approximately	approx.	minimum	min.
because	∵	minus	–
compare	cf.	number	no. or #
decrease	↘	pages	pp.
different from/unlike	≠	regarding	re
for example	e.g.	results from	←
government	govt	results in/leads to	→
greater than/more than	>	same as/ditto	"
important	imp.	similar to	≈
in other words, namely	i.e.	therefore	∴
increase	↗	versus	vs.
information	info.	very	v.
less than/smaller than	<	with reference to	re
like/equal to	=		

Appendix 2: Definitions of words used in this guide

academically rigorous sources Material that had been checked by experts (peer-reviewed) before publication.

acknowledge To indicate that a source has been used and to give information on that source. A common way of acknowledging an author is to give a reference (see below).

article A separate piece of writing in a larger publication. Common types of articles are newspaper articles, magazine articles and articles in academic journals.

baseless assertion A claim or statement that is not true and/or not supported by evidence.

cite, to To mention (and usually give information on) an author. A common way of citing is to give a reference. The word citation is also sometimes used to mean a quotation.

close paraphrase A use of source material with only minor word changes.

paraphrase A re-expressing and rewording of source material.

reference Information about a source. You give a reference in your assignment (an in-text reference) and also in your reference list.

source synthesis The combining and integrating of material and ideas from multiple sources to form a new argument or idea.

References

Godfrey J (2020) *The Student Phrase Book: Vocabulary for Writing at University* (2nd edn). London: Bloomsbury.

Godfrey J (2022) *Writing for University* (3rd edn). London: Bloomsbury.

Godwin J (2018) *Studying with Dyslexia* (2nd edn). London: Bloomsbury.

Godwin J (2019) *Planning your Essay* (3rd edn). London: Bloomsbury.

Lia P (2020) *Simplify your Study: Effective Strategies for Coursework and Exams*. London: Bloomsbury.

Mangen A Walgermo BR and Brønnick K (2013) Reading linear texts on paper versus computer screen: effects on reading comprehension. *International Journal of Educational Research*, 58: 61–8.

Rayner K, Schotter ER, Masson ME, Potter MC and Treiman R (2016) So much to read, so little time: How do we read, and can speed reading help? *Psychological Science in the Public Interest*, 17 (1): 4–34.

Williams K (2022) *Getting Critical* (3rd edn). London: Bloomsbury.

Williams K and Davis M (2017) *Referencing and Understanding Plagiarism* (2nd edn). London: Bloomsbury.

Index